PRAISE FOR *LEARNING TO DROWN*

"The speakers in *Learning to Drown* keep looking for ways to cope with experience that ranges from dismal to torturous—in a world where 'agony appears to be its own reward.' One speaker refers to 'the pale spirit of our daily crucifixion'—another knows too well 'the long chain of hollow hours.'

"It's a world of guilt and remorse—'each of us sent to beg forgiveness from whichever / gods we recognize while death patiently paces / the sky.' In this book even the efforts toward relief have an ominous quality: 'Take happiness seriously wherever / you find it, in beers made of lemongrass / or cocktails with elaborate names ...'

"Still, there is the happiness of language; the poems keep offering sentences that are sharp-edged and smart and bravely vivid. We can hope that poetry itself is a path out of dismay."

> — Mark Halliday
> author of *Keep This Forever, Thresherphobe*
> and *Losers Dream On*

LEARNING TO DROWN

Published by Gunpowder Press
Edited by David Starkey and Chryss Yost
PO Box 60035
Santa Barbara, CA 93160-0035

Front cover image by Annette McIntosh Stubbs

ISBN-13: 978-1-957062-19-8

Library of Congress Control Number: 2024922944

www.gunpowderpress.com

Gunpowder Press is part of Gunpowder Poetry, a 501(c)(3) nonprofit
literary organization.

LEARNING TO DROWN

POEMS

SM STUBBS

GUNPOWDER PRESS • SANTA BARBARA
2025

Contents

THREE.

For in tremendous extremities human souls are like drowning men; well enough they know they are in peril; well enough they know the causes of that peril; nevertheless, the sea is the sea, and these drowning men do drown.

— *Herman Melville*

ONE.

Oubliette

Across the block the bagel shop's neon blinks
Open... Open... Open... while up the sidewalk snow

coats blue and yellow tulips for sale at a bodega.
In a few hours each flower will look the same.

Everything I see reminds me of one specific rotation
of the earth 40 years ago. I don't understand

how this memory persists, an insistent, infinite loop
dreamt up by Escher, one of his drawings

where staircases lead back to their own landings.
That night is a flame on a candle that won't quit

and I don't know why. It burns steady as a sun
behind my ribs. I doubt a jury would find me guilty.

I've met Zen masters who say it doesn't matter,
that I locked myself away years ago and may never

jigsaw my way out. They say, *Forget yourself.*
I say, *Believe me, I never stop trying.* At times

that night is a moon heavy with tides and
I don't know why. It tugs at my rivers and lakes,

floods my shorelines twice a day. Stars ghost
and glare off the uneven roofs of the brownstones

along Hicks, off the semis haunting the BQE.
I'm trapped in this black and white landscape

where my hands bend to draw themselves, where
birds become fish and fish forever become birds.

Asylum Sleight of Hand

In order to escape you must know the sounds
      for *trap* and *fettered flesh*. You must allow yourself

to be audacious, a name for a type of dare. This
      is a lesson in embracing the other. To start with,

stop apologizing for the spoiled hull of your body.
      Next, learn to get away with what doesn't belong

to you: starlight, the smell of jasmine, the weight
      of hollow bones called a wing. Death is either

reprieve or release. When our judgment ends
      we are free to never eat, never sleep, never learn

the geometry of any lover's extended sentence,
      their pliable curves and neon stitches. Do you

have the nerve? A lab on the south of town
      proves that risk-taking is good for our health,

that it energizes us like a fresh set of electrodes.
      Whatever holds you eventually loosens its grip.

Learning to Shut Up

I do not yet know the words for hands
on my body though I need to tell my parents
about the man's rough palms. I am eight. It's hot.
We slide into the Lincoln on our way to dinner.
I need to tell them where we were
without clothes, how often. I ask if I'm allowed
to speak. "Of course," they say, but my voice
is an ember I can't stoke into flame.
I don't yet know how to describe the electricity
bodies contain, haven't learned that sex
is a language with its own set of exceptions.
My eyes scan the Billy Joel cassettes scattered
along the back seat. I don't notice track 8
from *Piano Man*, "If I Only Had the Words (To Tell You)"
and even if I did a song is never as terrible
as the real thing. I'm fixated
by the cover of a different Billy Joel album,
The Stranger: he's curled up on an unmade bed,
a pair of boxing gloves hang from a hook
and a hollow mask rests on the pillow. How
do I explain that I too feel hollow, that their world
has provided no context for my seared flesh?
The air swelters late on that Florida afternoon.
My parents wait, limned in dusk light.
Track 6, "Only the Good Die Young." I wonder,
suddenly, if I'm good. I wonder if I will be if I describe
shades of pale skin against more pale skin.
The man told me not to breathe a word. The man told me
silence is golden. I am good and don't want to die
but I do want to break each of his fingers
and watch how he suffers. I just don't know yet
how to forge these unfamiliar sounds;
I don't know how to make my parents listen
when I open this furnace.

The Elephants

Hannibal's army in the Alps in November,
elephants struggling up unfamiliar iced paths
months from the African plains.
Elephants in the Alps, and the locals
who would not attack the ranks of soldiers
upon seeing those massive beasts. Elephants need
four hundred pounds of food
and thirty to fifty gallons of water, per day.

⊙

I'm in a café. Across from me a woman sips coffee.
She lights a cigarette, smokes it,
lights another. She's looking at nothing.
She reminds me in no specific way
of a girl I knew at church, how she moves
when she decides what she wants,
how she smiles with her eyes.

⊙

Herr Ober brings water and asks
if I'd like a piece of cake? No thank you.
He frowns. It's Sunday. Everyone eats cake on Sunday.
No, please, I'm obsessed: the African bush elephant
is the largest land mammal in the world.
A large male, or bull, may weigh
six tons or more.
Females are generally smaller.

⊙

This woman reminds me
of the night you stripped for me,
you, the daughter of family friends.
Your parents were having a party,
we were in your room playing pick-up-stix.
Suddenly you shut yourself in your closet,
began tossing out clothes. I saw a flash
that was your hip before you stopped, dressed,
made me finish our game. My mother tells me
you went wrong, whatever that means,
that after years of arrests and running away
every other month you finally lost yourself
up north, misplaced on the streets
of one of the great cities, though which one
no one knows for sure.
I'm not certain what any of this
has to do with elephants.

◉

It could be that I'm thinking how displaced
they were, how easily one
might've gone missing. Records claim
that of the thirty-seven Hannibal drove from Africa, not one died.
For some reason I don't believe that.
For example, where in the winter Alps could they find
eight tons of hay and straw? That can't be easy.
One of the elephants must've slipped,
delirious with hunger, or thirst, must've
stepped wrong off the path causing
a minor avalanche. Yes. One catastrophic and
chaotic afternoon, injuries sustained by their handlers, one
of the bulls plunged down a steep slope

gathering debris as the mountainside crumbled
beneath its weight. Think
of those tusks cracking against rocks,
that carcass still as a dome.
And the villagers, afraid at first, tentative to touch,
would revere that grey-eared thing
until it began to rot.
And later as the flesh dripped away
all that was left was an outline, a hint of something huge—
a giant barrel, the hull of a boat—
covered in snow six months out of the year.

⊙

I'm not sitting in this café thinking of elephants
because you've disappeared. No.
It's from long before that, even before the night
you didn't quite strip.
                                    Our parents
have gone out to dinner and we're left
in the hands of Frank, my usual sitter.
Elephants, in the Alps.
The woman sipping coffee is beautiful.
                                    Frank
has discussed this moment with me
and is prepared with a camera
          which of course has no film.
                    I don't want to write
what I'm thinking.
                    The woman
                              sipping coffee
                                        is beautiful.
Frank claims he's a photographer
                    for Playboy,

pulls out the latest issue.
The woman
lights her third cigarette
with gestures which suggest
she could destroy me.
Frank suggests
we take some pictures.
The bull's trunk flails
as it plummets. Its ears snap.
We're not even nine.
Frank is eighteen.
I'm hungry for the chance
to be shattered.
You agree to take off
your shirt.
Now her lips—
their shape, the way they flutter—
You are in
your underwear.
There are elephants
in the Alps. A beauty mark
near her left eye.
Finally
you are bare: flat-chested, without hips,
slightly rounded belly. Frank praises you
and removes his socks. I do the same.
In minutes, the three of us stand naked before the camera
set up across the room,
you sandwiched between us.
Frank makes absurd clicking noises,
mimics the sound of the shutter as if it has a timer.
We barely pretend anymore.

9

My erection
   is a twig next to his. After more
        of this posing
I'm kicked out of the room.
      Elephants.
One lost in the snow.
     Its tusks strike rocks and then
that awful silence
   when the avalanche
is finished, and the sound
      of pebbles spilling down,
pitting the tusks,
    chipping them,
        that click
    I keep hearing.
The woman sipping coffee
      gets up and leaves.
All I hear
    for the next thirty minutes,
  watching the door,
staring out the windows,
      listening
for clues to what's going on,
       is Frank's tongue
ticking
   against the roof of his mouth.

Asylum Linguistics

It turns out the word "fornicate" used to mean
       an arched or vaulted form, as if two bodies

bent by heat could carry the weight of the sky.
       One root suggests "brothel," another means

a "domed shape" or "covered way." Roman
       prostitutes solicited business under the arches

of certain buildings which is why one author
       of the bible linked the location to adultery.

I'd ask him about the importance of contact,
       skin to skin, the manner in which we most

reveal ourselves. I'd ask him if he knew how
       to define love or the four elements of a fractured

selfhood. I'd tell him: we are poisoned through
       our mouths, the center of half our sins. Without

evidence we don't really know what we know.
       How far will we fall? As far as language allows.

Undone

For seven years I've been trapped
in the grinding gear of dive-bar cocktails
and changing kegs and slicing fruit
yet when I have a minute to pause
my eyes linger on the drinkers
along the cinder-block walls
the long steel drink rails and worn
wooden bar and when I recognize
the cage I've made I think
Undo this, undo this and no
I don't mean tonight's ninth
Tequila Sour or Tom Collins but
the times as a boy I stayed awake
on school nights rehashing
the sequence of moments when flesh
led me to other flesh and in that darkness
discovered blame and shame
were twin cogs installed at birth
machined to function whether or not
I wanted them to and I can never
undo this, undo this and yes
I'd love to disappear to any spot
stocked with carts of sweets
that won't stop my heart I mean
it could be Yakutsk or Nepal or even
one of the moon's secluded craters
and still I would never be enough
miles or years away to unhear
that silky insistence as he smiles
at the girl then winks at me
and convinces her to
Undo this, undo this and then
what happened after.

Asylum Schedule

They keep changing the day I'm awake in:
        now it's Thursday and I'm handed pamphlets

to read and comprehend. Their fascination
        with the limits of pain never ends: *Does this hurt?*

Yes. *And this?* Again, yes. Again, again, again.
        And yet I gain nothing. They say it will only

last a minute, can't see how each second
        becomes its own eternity. At one time *agony*

meant a sudden display of joy or delight. From
        the Greek, *agon*: a struggle or contest for a prize.

Do you smell smoke, or taste it? Do you suffer
        from night terrors? Can you quantify your joy

as a prime number? The world smudges into
        watercolors if I don't sleep for too many days.

That's when my face melts in the mirror
        and the sun becomes a songbird on fire.

Spiritual

Spring mist sashays off the river
as we clap and sing single file down the bank.
In the water our gowns go translucent
and our skin's so thin we watch
each other's hearts beat. When
it's our turn we're plunged backwards,
held under so long we wonder if air
will fill our lungs again or if being filled
with eternal love will suffice. Is this
the test we were told to expect?
Before our throats seize we're gasping
at the gift of breath in our mouths.
Now we are sanctified, saved.
The older saints warm our skin
and whisper: have faith in the river,
in the mist, in those that lead us
toward light. We shudder while
the herald holds friends and family
under, each beneath the water longer
than the one before, the *hosannas* loud enough
to shock the guards at the gates of Heaven.
All morning the shepherd shocks faith
into his people. We cheer again and again,
louder each time they almost drown.

Asylum Tonight

In the purple zone I am royalty, leniently treated.
        This is along the corridor of smudged plum

where King George haunts the day room and
        Ludwig of Bavaria keeps building castles. Flashes

strobe outside windows as bullets shaped like
        raindrops *pop!* Someone hands me a candle, thinks

my clothes won't ignite, thinks it means an end
        to darkness. Voices shuffle across tiles. When

the screaming game begins even the paint on the walls
        hurts my skin. It doesn't matter if I don't know

what's real, a fluorescent flick watches over me.
        Some nights it hums hymns; some nights this cell

expands like a lung. I may have a fever. I may
        reenact my own burning man. I have a story to tell

starring the silhouetted trees beyond the fence.
        At sundown they fracture the fine sky with cracks.

Tender

For five days straight a man
settles on the same worn stool,
peels an orange, eats each
segment between sips
of the same brand of beer
he drank the day before.
A single hour to recall
who he used to be or to forget
whatever leaves a scar.
The rest of the week
he scrapes his knuckles
against machine parts and
the dashboard of his truck.
He feels like a ghost
pouring itself into a stranger.
He feels like a song
no one has ever heard.
Summer again and that heat
it hurts to breathe is the only thing
he remembers ever wanting.

Waking Up in Florida

Water from a sprinkler
hits the window every twenty-seven
seconds. A mockingbird rises
and falls along the power lines running
through the back yard. She sings,
lifts into the air then settles
again. After that, freight trains
loaded with products bound
for South America chug toward Miami,
traffic hisses coolly on US 1
and semis floor it up and down I-95.
Late in the afternoon a catalog
of other birds and the hum
of airborne insects. I hear those
before waves collapsing on shore
or whitecaps smacking
the bow of the boat.
It's my childhood, noises
outside the house louder than
memory, louder than my voice
crashing against the walls,
its paper-thin buzz
like a dragonfly trapped
on a screened-in porch.

Asylum Meditation

End of summer and the air boils. Moths
        fluster the street lights as a classic song

drifts from a rooftop down by the river.
        Reading ancient Chinese poets, I discover

I too am filled with a longing for what
        no longer belongs to me. Tonight, the moon

is a mirror, look how we sound in it.
        I don't know what I'm supposed to ask

of the world anymore. Whatever it was,
        it's gone, swung like a pendulum in sand,

the big one in the museum that proves
        gravity or perpetual motion. Wait—what

I thought was a voice was only the breeze
        as it blew past our windows. How lucky

to be stunned into silence by a night sky
        filled with notes sung by so many suns.

Déjà Vu

Light flickers like it does in dreams, quick hits
of darkness, long enough to feel anxious.
The bartender refills my glass before

I ask. She cuts lemons into wedges
then cuts lemons into wedges. No one
notices we've heard this song already—

haven't we? Maybe more than once. I know
the lushes seated nearby. Not their names
or personal histories, but I've seen

their faces fill with grace and mercy. Each
struggles daily with their own untamed faith.
I need help. I can't recall why this song

repeats or why I'm dizzy now, weeping
over a tune I can't seem to forget.

Learning to Drown

Sounds counter intuitive, says the instructor,
but to know how to prevent it, we have to experience it
ourselves. He refers to *breath-hold time* and how
swim failure may take hours, how quickly the process
moves. First instinct: you struggle to keep
your airway clear of water. This phase
always takes less than sixty seconds.
Second instinct: as you submerge, you hold
your breath as long as you can. Third?
Aspiration, which means you've inhaled fluids.
He tells us to begin our efforts before phase three,
that jumping in is the last resort and so,
for an hour, we practice the use of life preservers,
ropes, paddles, oars, brooms, we improvise
with anything that extends our reach without
putting ourselves in harm's way. The drowning
will try to use us as flotation devices and then we both die.
He rattles off statistics: 80% of drowning victims
are below the age of twenty; 80% are male;
67% of drownings are nonfatal which means
someone was there to save them.

The next day, we practice removing clothes
and shoes in under twenty seconds. We enter the water
feet first, head first, then by jumping in wearing
every stitch to feel the weight of wet clothes.
Finally, we take turns pretending to drown.
Half tread water in the dark Loxahatchee
while the rest prepare to save us. As victims,

we're told to go after our saviors, to grab them
by the neck, flail about, splash water in their eyes.
The lifeguard should approach from behind.
When the victims' backs are turned, slide an arm
under theirs and across their chest, this establishes
control and keeps their head above water.
Do not try to reason with the victim; logic
has no meaning for the dying. Time
will move in deep, still pulses. The shore
will feel miles away. For two hours
the class tried to save me. First one Scout,
then two, then the instructor. I took my drowning
seriously and fought them as instructed.
In all that time no one managed to work out
how to keep me from going under.

Asylum Testament

History is how we're tethered to certain
   stretches of land. The minute you're kissed

or punched, you and that place own each other.
   Sometimes I want to wipe a small town off

the map. I want to be so Old Testament I get
   to choose my own plagues. I've been resident

at this address longer than anywhere else,
   the mess is how I know it's okay to breathe.

When biological defenses outpace our common
   sense, the result is fear—everything heightened

by the need to cut things open. Blood suggests
   rebirth and the sharpest blades. When opening

this bible you'll find the Gospel of Mutilations,
   in which dismemberments turn into a holiday

dance. I know the graphic violence is hard to take
   but at least hang on through the blizzard.

TWO.

Porch Song

We're at Chad's place after shift, sitting
in plastic lawn chairs on the porch. He's spitting dip
into a Styrofoam cup, his bare feet up
against the rail. We're drinking Michelob.
The sun's fading into leaves of oak across the street,
early August hot and slow. Chad rubs liniment in
where his forearm brushed the restaurant's toaster,
his latest kitchen scar. Nothing new for us,
tips of my fingers long gone smooth,
nerve-ends melted from grabbing trays
out of the oven, bread off the grill. He mutters
how his girlfriend keeps giving him hell
about new paint for the siding and window frames,
other chores left unfinished. We talk shop,
about the old cook freaking out high again
and how the night manager won't have Chad over
to her house where she's got not one but two
confectioner's ovens as well as all the pots
he needs for his dream diner. He tells me again
about the mountains in India and still can't believe
I ran the table on him at the pool hall earlier.
It has only been a couple of months and it's as if
we've known each other always, the brother
we each never had. The talk turns
to favorite books and he wonders why
there aren't more things written about guys drinking
after work, sun going down, watching flies
gather in the shade of a wooden swing,
how they plague the rough bone he gave his dog
the day before, how they pester the dog's seeping eyes,

and then a dozen black birds settle
on the oak's lower branches away from the heat.
He wipes condensation off the bottle in his hand
and says I should write about these droplets
spilling onto the plain pine boards,
slowly soaking in, spots turning to vapor
until they're no longer visible.

Bottomless Cup

The woman behind the counter says
Sing into my mouth and I repeat my request
for maple syrup. The pancakes stacked
next to a wan wedge of fruit
aren't going to sweeten themselves.
Go ahead, she insists, *it's okay*.
I'm neither throat surgeon nor dentist.
I don't feel comfortable this close
to another open mouth but now
people are watching. I take a breath,
lean over, spool out half a verse
of the Eagles' "One of These Nights."
Seconds later my words ricochet back
as if her chest contains a canyon
or some vast, drafty cave: *one of these
crazy old nights...* The regulars cackle.
Katie bows, pats me on the shoulder,
shrugs. A look of pride and resignation
vibrates behind her eyes. I realize how easy
it would be to fall in love with someone
who knows the secrets of air and
the importance of endless pots of coffee.
I smother my food, cut, chew.
When she takes other customers' orders
I hear traces of every diner she ever worked in
and sly hints of the cheap, sorry stiffs
who never understood the mystery,
those vacant singers who couldn't stand
to spend years listening to the echo
of their own weak, diminished voices.

Up in This Trailer Park

Three of us at the bar playing Uno, me,
Jimmy and Mike, the only ones starting early
while on the stereo the Misfits kept
reminding us to *Die! Die!* When they went out
to smoke with the bartender, I was alone,
could have robbed the till if I'd wanted
even though I'd lose the embrace of a place
I'd grown comfortable, would have to let go
of friendships hatched after five or six pints.
They came back, we kept playing. The day-shift
went home and Jimmy started pounding his drinks.
As dusk settled, we had to tilt our cards
toward the stuttering candlelight to determine
which were blue and which were green.
Others trickled in, Jimmy made less sense
by the minute, shouting, *I'm gonna whoop some ass*
up in this trailer park! I need more beer up in
this trailer park! – cackling every time he said it.
In many ways, a bar is similar to places
you'd park a mobile home, a barstool
another type of temporary residence.
We promise ourselves we can leave any time
while the axles rust and the wheels deflate
a little more every month. This is one of the ways
we find stopgap homes for ourselves,
how we almost never choose our neighbors
or even what light we park under. None of us
is going to forget death is coming just like
nobody hooks their cables to any place
they don't think they can wake up in.
One day you open your eyes and know exactly
where you are. You put on a shirt, venture
outside. Someone waves, offers coffee or beer.
You hold what's in front of you and sip.

Viewer's Guide to Masculinity in Three Films

Perhaps someone you know is a man
or you yourself are and would like to know more.
Rent *Shaun of the Dead*, *Hot Fuzz*, and *The World's End*,
the films in Edgar Wright's Cornetto Trilogy.
Note how they're a complex study

in friendship, that Simon Pegg and Nick Frost
star in all three. Observe the dynamic:
they drink and kill zombies; they drink
and fight the neighborhood watch alliance;
they drink and destroy aliens. Next, pay attention

to how pubs, fences and twins reverberate
throughout: pubs equal shared community; fences
represent obstacles; twins are simply a creepy mirroring
of the best-friend pair as they go about
the business of saving our world.

Being someone's best friend can feel like
you're saving the world. At this point, have a drink.
Beer is preferred, shots of whiskey permitted
or, really, anything you can drown in.
These relationships rely on the easy confidence

found in alcohol. Men say nothing until suddenly
we are vulnerable in loud ways.
Who hasn't found themselves weeping at 2 a.m.
over the kitchen counter of someone
as intimate as a second self? When the time comes,

hold your best friend in your arms
as the two of you die, or might, and pray
for another close call, one more last-second miracle
and please note what you might have had to do
if you didn't have each other to carry into tomorrow.

Hunt Camp, Labelle, FL

There's talk of natural disasters,
eclipses, full moons shining bright
off the soft sugar sand and scrub pines.
There's the sound of more bottles popped open
and *Shit, I can't believe it*. Everyone stares,
some smile shyly, ask to stroke
the thin, straight horns of a gazelle
roped onto a jeep. In the parking lot,
there's at least one deer strapped to each truck,
rifles and shotguns on window racks,
men who suckle beers and shuffle
from one tall tale to another. It is dusk.
They're all sore from squatting in trees
and pissing in bottles since well before sunrise.
Minutes later some new car pulls in,
a grizzly tied to the top, its fur wet and pulpy.
It's set up there like a Christmas tree.
Then an El Camino arrives with
an elephant poured in back like cement.
Now they're all speechless and wide-eyed
and don't notice the Land Rover
with a llama poking out the back,
don't know there's a flatbed on the way
with Livingstone at the wheel,
a stegosaurus shot through the head
plowing like the figure on the prow
of an ancient seventeenth-century schooner.
You shoulda seen the one that got away, boys.
There's a tremor in the distance, a roar
through the dark, a flood of birds taking wing
and raccoons clearing out, the pulse
of trees and leaves flying— there's that
new electric throb in the coarse cool air.

Wanting to Be a Fish

Because other kids held their breath longer
      than I could, I wanted gills. In my parents'
            bathroom I found a razor blade and sliced my neck

three times on the left side. Before I could do
      the rest my father's rage swept me up, a tsunami
            of parental panic. He pressed a towel hard against

my throat and I choked, his hands tense tides
      pinning me to the passenger seat of his Lincoln.
            I bled all over the aisle of the drugstore where

he wound me with gauze. True, it was hard
      to stay calm without oxygen, his bandages tied
            tourniquet-tight, but the worst part was his look,

a mix of anger and something I still can't read.
      At the time, I thought he hated me for doing
            something stupid that could have been avoided

had I realized how much trouble it would be
      for him to save me. I thought he'd rather have
            a son who stuck to the shallows and never wondered

what it was like to swim to the horizon
      where the ocean's so deep it simply disappears.

Armistice

The boy in the yard wages war
with molded soldiers. Green plastic
for the US, grey for the Germans.
Slender palms bend and wave nearby.
The boy gestures to one army then
the other. Negotiations commence,
a peace accord guaranteeing zero losses
for either side. There will be no blood
today, and now they've decided
to throw a dance party with a mosh pit
where they'll mingle and pledge to do no harm
to one another. It's the Christmas truce
of 1914 from the First World War,
only with more glitter and disco music.
The boy enjoys staging the battles
but prefers his world at peace, harmony
flooding the air like gas, nothing lost
or quietly raging. They're given minutes
to relax, recuperation in the form
of shaking and wriggling in the tall grass.

Devo Begs a Question

Are we not men? I'm no longer certain.
According to their first album, they are Devo—
but what about the rest of us? We aren't
equipped with amps and electric guitars
and outfits like demented spacemen.
I catalog these feet and knees, lips and heart,
a decent start, but what makes us not just
male, but *men*? When we were kids,
my friend bought the Devo album
around the time I began to notice music
and I had to have it, too. My own, not one
of dad's cassettes scattered on the car floor:
Billy Joel, Earth, Wind & Fire, Little River Band.
I studied the album liner notes for answers
as their question nested in my brain:
if we weren't men, were there options? If
I could be anything, it would be a platypus,
the ultimate defier of categories, capable
of claiming roots in multiple species.
I told my college orientation pod
that this strange animal best described how
I saw myself. For four years they greeted me
as *flightless-avian-mammal-man*. I don't know
how to answer Devo's question and
want to be more than merely a man—
more grace, more light, more generous
with my affections. I suspect we're already
surrounded by those who've evolved
or were always more, but simply hid it:
no wings, no halo, no holy spirit
beaming from behind the eyes, yet love
and mercy fall upon me often enough
that I have to wonder: are they not angels?
Perhaps, some of them, are they not?

The Spoils

The thing is, you have Paris and California
and all I have is this bird. It shits
non-stop, and when I said
I wanted to remember you, I meant
your mouth scented with wine and your calves
as they tipped you up to kiss me and even
the embrace of your sighs. It may be
too much to ask, I know. I left you
the stereo and big-screen TV; I left you
the Polish landlord who loved wrestling; I left you
the platform bed you never really liked—
and not one of those defecates in your cereal.
Justice isn't made to partner love. None of this
is how it was meant to go. There were times
we held each other when there was nowhere else
in the world, but that was long ago.
Now I'm nauseous twenty-four seven
and my dreams twitch with the metal twang
of your chinchillas in their cages, so many
sleepless nights. There are days when I wish
this bird had been a vampire bat with plans
to drain me of vital essences. There are other days
when I wish it was a Guanay cormorant—
their feces tend to explode. Either way
I imagine me up after midnight scraping guano
from the furniture and floors, learning
how to extract the potassium nitrate, me burning
our table and chairs for charcoal. I imagine
buying sulfur at the garden center,
mixing it in a huge bucket.
I take that crude gunpowder and lace
our past with it. I strike a match, prepared
to fly. I let the flame go and act like those fireworks
have nothing to do with love, or ruin, or me.

Quarantine Binge-Watching

Movies we knew by heart followed by
the tiger guy followed by a sequence
of BBC mysteries including forty-six seasons
of village murders and the histories of castles
and any low-budget game show
where people fall into lava or mud. After that
we spent nights tuned in and out as long
as my guy had product and I can't remember
May at all. I'm certain it happened
but whichever dreams bathed us
in their digital gleam have been lost
to pandemic anxiety. This is our routine now
Monday to Sunday and we're halfway through
the baking show for a third time: someone
ruins their pastry, someone fails to make
their chocolate shine, and so on. I know this
the way I know a virus can live forever.

Days, I study my Sibley Guide to Birds
trying to match the artist's renderings
with the winged things in the trees out back,
translating art back into reality. At night
I try not to think about the news
or my aging parents or the tragedies none of us
can put a stop to. Instead, I escape
inside the screen to anywhere peaceful.
England's nice, in spite of the bizarre deaths.
Everyone seems polite and implausibly cordial
and unlikely to breathe contagions on me.
Perhaps later, when this has ended,

we'll find a spot in a quaint village to move to,
maybe a stone house where people once
threw pots or repaired antiques, where
I could watch the lavender grow
and ignore the insistent rasp of this world.

Gothic

Upon a hill, a house. Upon the house,
a roof. On the roof, a bird. The bird—
oiled feathers, beak like an awl—grooms
the roof's moss, subsists on ticks
and silverfish. Inside the house, a man
without a tongue and a woman
who loves him. The woman grooms
the house, subsists on potatoes and rice
and whatever rodents roam the slope.
The man hunts every day until noon.
Every day he returns empty-handed,
his shoulders tense as flywheels,
his jaw the floor of a collapsed cave,
crowded with everything he cannot say.
She brews his tea. She washes the corners
of the house. She chases the bird away.
At sundown the man leaves again, hunting.
Upon another hill, another house. Another
woman waits inside. The man without
a tongue feasts on rabbit she trapped
in a pit. From fireplace ashes she makes lye
and scrubs his back. She fills his canteen with it.
By the time her sister misses him, his body
has sunk to the bottom of the pond.

Upstate

I'm not sure what to say about that night
at Vic's Tavern, a quarter-mile from the weekend
rental house, or hours earlier, the fire pit
the four of us huddled around, scalding our knees,
our gloved hands clamped around beers in the icy mist

of a twenty-seven-degree Saturday in April.
Our hair and jeans reeked of smoke and when
we couldn't take the chill we went to the town's only bar.
We shot pool 'til one of us sank the eight ball on the break
and it wasn't long before the regulars crowded in.

I think often of the couple throwing their fists
at the electric punching bag for an hour straight,
bloodying their knuckles again and again
against the AIM HERE circle. I'm not sure
what to say about the drunk who called my friends

a bunch of jagoffs when they wouldn't take their turns
throwing the punches he'd spotted us
on that machine. I'll remember the mounted buck
with taxidermied fangs and how the patrons
clustered, none of them a day over twenty-five,

the men shadows in work clothes looming over
their high-school sweethearts, each sizing
the others up, how more and more appeared as the night
went on, shifts ending hourly around the county,
until they silently side-eyed us into leaving.

As we hurried back we heard a sound rise
off the frozen Sacandaga River, a loud piercing moan
riding the wind of the incoming ice storm,
and couldn't decide if it was the frostbitten trees
or the restless floes caught between the banks.

Tech-Friendly Apocalypse

What someone manages to broadcast on television
will help keep us alive. Behind barricaded doors

we'll lose ourselves in reruns, feast on corn and rice
scavenged from deserted farms. We'll sew scraps

of lace into delicate shawls to remind the world
it wasn't always rubble and the stench of burnt meat.

No one knows who erected the solar cells but thanks
to them I dream about a hundred pastries I'll never

eat again, relive historic battles so basic they look like
kids with sticks. A vision: one night we're sharing

soup with strangers at an old diner. We sip gin made
in a neighbor's bathtub and go blind as someone

nearby dies from what wasn't killed in the boil.
The half-life of fallout makes everyone untouchable.

Tonight, let's watch lewd movies on a loop and relive
memories of our nearly-perfect skin. After sundown

we'll generate the current that draws body to body,
an electricity that scorches before it slides into joy.

Aftermath

Each body broken, violet wounds, ash,
bullets like fireflies, dozens of caskets
weighted with clay unmade by misplaced rage.

Mourning continues as a vacant ache,
an absence heavier than upturned dirt
while the body's a miracle of dust

and lightning. Yes, I would like to be scorched
under the umbrella of you tonight,
can't wait to burn with the mercy of your

fevered kisses. Please reduce me to soot.
Please use me to mark the doltish faces
of those who would deny we are dying

or show me how to twist grief's thick neck
into a shield I carry through the world.

In the Town That Talks to the Dead

I. Us

We bring baskets of deviled eggs and ham,
whatever the dead might miss. We cling
to photos of loved ones, set chairs in a circle,
wait for the tug. We're searching for what
we've lost, pieces of our hearts stolen

by death. For my many recent losses
I want to know if the dead heal, if they feel heat
through the veil, if they're given explanations.
I don't believe one god made all this suffering.
Or these scars. Or this sunburnt flesh.

A deity should have no patience for misery,
that's what we were taught. The wind
howls like collapsed lungs; we close our sweaters
against the cold. They are amongst us.

II. Them

The lack of a body, its battle with gravity,
this we like about our place. The lack of
a body, no sudden pulse in the gut at the flick
of wet lips, this we hate about our place.
Memories never stop unraveling, a lazy fade.

You may not know us. Or we may be ghosts
of ancestors who committed murder

to feed the gaping maw that ends with your face.
It won't help you to know this: eternity
is a maze with walls of breath and weeping.

All is dark. We have met no gods. If they
exist, there is none so cruel as we are
to each other. We cannot say if this is Heaven
or a wound there will never be a cure for.

Café in Early Winter

A rumpled coat of a man taps his toes
against the legs of a cramped corner table.
He has circles of sweat under his arms.
The cuff on his pants is too short,
his shoes scuffed and worn.
He places his order and watches
a well-dressed woman move toward him.
At the next table another woman stands
to greet her. They appear to be old friends.
The man pays attention out the sides of his eyes,
pupils darting toward them like a metronome.
He thanks the waiter for his coffee, drops
three sugars in and doesn't know what to do
with his hands. After each sip he stares
into the cup, searching the bottom.
He folds a sugar wrapper,
unfolds it, rolls it into a tiny tube,
imagines greeting and hugging those
coming in. He can nearly hear their laughter
as he tells his latest stories. He reads
a paper left by another customer.
Throughout the afternoon he anticipates
a shift into allegro, the tempo change
that signifies action with closure.
The women at the next table
share another piece of cake.
It is dark out when the man leaves,
streetlights almost warm enough to shine.

Time and Tide

The lunar mountain Mons Huygens
was named for the Dutchman who invented
the pendulum clock, which is the way
most of us learned that time does not sit still.
Yes, flowers blossom and they also die. Yes,
the sea approaches and also recedes. We can build
a fort out of books and wine bottles,
live like royalty, yet the structure
will collapse. I want to take our pain
to a chapel and sit in a pew until I'm certain
the silence filling the rafters means
our deities have stopped listening. In the eyes
of any omniscient we must be nothing.
Next to a million solar systems? Less
still. Next to an infinity of supernovas?
We are the pulse of animated carbon,
seven billion microscopic black holes.
Minor, minuscule. From a god's point of view
our differences indistinguishable.
Days sway against days.

THREE.

Hammerstein Ballroom

Last night at the Anthrax concert the boys
angry on crap beer they paid too much for
broke their bodies against each others' bodies.

The rest of the crowd nodded in time, horns
up, waves of sound slicing into our jeans.
Everyone wore black, which is the camouflage

of frustration and fury. The guys in the band
have finally gotten old. Their fans, too.
At one point a glassy-eyed washout wrecked

on a reef of chemicals and booze flopped
off a woman in front of us and fell into
my surprised arms. I cradled his head as we sank

to the floor. Foam lined the corners of his
mouth while Security shouted into their radios.
As his eyes rolled back I could see nothing

but a jetty of veins and a thousand nights
just like this one. They strapped him
into a wheeled chair and he was gone.

We got home after midnight and pried open
bottles of beer we'd been saving—good stuff—
then watched on TV as thirty sailfish slashed

a school of bait into a red, shimmering frenzy.

Asylum Release

We're scarred, but not all scars are created equal.
    It can be helpful to come at it from a surprising angle,

i.e., the wire caught in that branch is the same color
    as the wire he tied my hands with. Understand,

the heart wants to share its pain with another heart.
    If not share, inflict. This the blues. This

the stretched-out forever ahead. Dolor on the hi-fi,
    guitar and harmonies like a soul on fire. A loss.

A wound. A scab you carry inside. Bruises and lacerations
    are fine if inflicted at significant moments:

a lover's teeth, a father's belt buckle, a mother's wine glass
    opening the smooth landscape of your flesh.

In the empty after: the challenge of the body sacred.
    No one wants to ruin their childhood yet these thick

chains clatter with every step. First, you must admit
    the child you were wasn't sure what wanting meant.

Asylum: An Argument

I.

House: a family, firm or building
used as dwelling; domicile/residence/shelter.
Home: a place of origin; an institution
where people are cared for; wherever one resides.
For example, I reside in these arms,
these knees, these crooked teeth.
I am at home behind these eyes, this my castle,
this my asylum. The word *asylum* means refuge,
from the Greek, *asulon*: "a" meaning without
and "sulon" meaning right of seizure—
a place where you could not be seized.
Asulos means inviolable. In the late
14th century it was understood to mean,
"safe from violence." You could request *asylum*
and expect protection. When the home
is merely a house, how does it refuge?

II.

Where I was raised a man touched me.
That was a violation. He did it
more than once. Did I break? I wanted to.
When he took the girl into my bedroom
and locked the door while I stood outside,
did I crush the eight cramped cells
of our weak hearts? We were neither inviolable
nor safe from violence. I shut myself in,
fled through unknown tunnels, hid
parts of me in places I've spent
every year since forgetting how to find.

I reside in this structure, am almost home
in this house. At night I wander the halls
tapping wood panels waiting to hear
that telltale hollow. I wonder
what I hid and where.

III.
I have begun to recognize my body
as an accumulation of rooms. After all,
my heart is made of chambers and my lungs
host formal balls where air dances in and out.
My stomach is a banquet hall beneath
the beams and rafters of my ribs. The apostle Paul
called the body a temple. Mine was built
for pagan gods. Blood's been spilled here,
alongside cases of bourbon, pints of ice cream.
My body *is* a house. Its attic contains
albums packed with photos, moments
fixed when there was cause to smile;
the garage is lined with fishing rods, power tools,
bicycles stalled by rusting chains, boxes of old clothes
used for dress-up. My body hosts pool parties,
pub crawls, book clubs. My body is pragmatic
with comfortable couches, springs spent,
upholstery in tatters. It needs
more repair every year.

IV.
Geheimgangsverlockung means
"secret-corridor-seduction" in German.
It's the idea that every old house contains
secret passages and yes I'm an old house

riddled with crawl spaces through which I shift
from one part of me to another. I've been hiding
for almost forty years. I'm the feral kid
in *Road Warrior* popping out of gopher holes.
I'm Bowie in *Labyrinth*, Alice's white rabbit,
a hobbit, a dwarf, an orc. I'm Gollum
posing riddles in the dark, hoping
I'll meet someone with answers.
My surfaces were scorched and I hid.
The scalding wind of what I can't recover from
blows and blows. In the literature of apocalypse
humans survive in warrens underground
and some never get a chance to see the sun.

Fortune

He strides the avenues
at ease, in love with the city
until he's forced to remember
nights his boyish body
was a pew where an older man
knelt and prayed. After that
the whole world's
off-kilter, seasons become
degrees of suffering:
spring's mild rashes, fall's
inflamed hips. The pain
he used to ignore
grows unbearable. The doctor
cannot find the problem,
tests reveal nothing.
He waits for angels or
demons, any spirit that will
guide him faithfully
and help him recall who
he was meant to be.

Asylum Trial

These confessions sum up what I need
        to say. Assemblymen meeting in the old stone

house will have these words and only these
        to distract them through winter. Some day

there will be a thaw. There will be a pulpit.
        Prayers spoken aloud, after which lesser

entreaties will be whispered. It will be nigh
        unto impossible to convict the perpetrator

yet the record must reflect. Specific elements
        of these crimes must be recorded, the more

salacious bits euphemized; exhibits B to G
        consisting mostly of graphic photographs,

redacted. The committee may find themselves
        unable to confront the evidence or unwilling

to fall asleep and dream knowing full well
        they've committed these same atrocities.

Asylum Sunday

If I tell you I have a map to the underworld
      with traps marked and circled in red and if

I tell you I mean to release the penitent, turn them
      into an army, would you forge our weapons?

Please involve bees because I love the idea
      of wielding a thousand stings. It is said that a dip

in the River Styx makes me invulnerable. If so
      I'll swim with my mouth open so my tongue

won't be the body that fails me. You assume when
      I say *sulfur* I'm going to say *brimstone*, that God's

wrath is a blade I can touch. Miles of cliffs tower
      over the far shore—one cannot enter unbroken.

The approach to Hell will scar me but I love
      to watch myself bleed. Soon I'll harvest the fury

of those who've atoned and been left behind,
      rally them as we swarm together from the depths.

Hunger, or, Excessive Sunlight Can Lead to Heatstroke Which Can Lead to Delirium and Hallucinations

A man storms into a house
near the Gulf Coast of Florida.
It's mid-afternoon late in summer,
he's distraught, weeping. A woman
in rubber gloves up to her elbows
stands at the sink, feels pain deep
in her chest. She had visions like this
when she was a girl. Those ended
in a field of pews beaded with rain
as if the church they'd peopled
disintegrated around them. She doesn't
fear the man because she has seen
how it ends. He crashes against walls
and collapses by the kitchen table.
His legs knock over chairs, threaten
a half-assembled puzzle. She fills a glass
with water, sets it on the floor.
Thunder ricochets in the distance.
His agonies bleed into the air the way
heat hovers over asphalt. For a moment
she wants to match his pain, wants to
set fire to the curtains and carpet
to see which of them Heaven
gathers home first. When it comes
the storm is sudden. Raindrops smack
against the roof like hymnals
dropped from a plane.

Asylum Devotion

Lately I'm desperate for salvation, perhaps
        a rack of engraved tablets that sets me free.

While cruising north on I-24 past Chattanooga
        and Clarksville out onto the great highways

of the Midwest, I hunt for desserts worthy
        of worship. I've never traveled through either

Kansas or Nebraska but I hear they know their pies.
        In the meantime, I'm trying to learn

how to invert myself, intestines draped around
        my shoulders like a prayer shawl. That would

make me the star attraction, gawkers' eyes fixed
        and wide as I pull my guts out one bend at a time.

Years ago in Vienna I toured a crypt stuffed
        with kings, queens and heirs, an entire dynasty

stacked against the walls of spare, cramped vaults,
        each casket quietly begging for attention.

Watching My Favorite Show I'm Inspired by the Youngest Daughter of the King Killed in Season One

In the final season she names the people
she plans to take revenge on. There are
so many I can't hold my breath
as long as she needs to recite them.
In that moment I wonder if I should train
with a master assassin? After all
I know what it costs to hold on to hate
even if my list has only one entry: the man
who molested me as a child. He isn't
the only person to cause pain or anguish
or years of guilt and shame, but he did break me
in ways I still don't understand. If I knew
where to look, I'd find him. And if
I found him I could knock on his door.
If he remembered me, he might be
thrown by my smile, have no clue
what was coming. It wouldn't change
a thing but my mother often said
it never hurts to try. By the time
he decided I wasn't a threat
it would be over. I've studied this girl
as she rewrote her story
and from her learned how to make certain
he didn't notice he was dead
until the air around him went still
and the world silent
while all he was
coursed in scarlet plumes
from his neck, eyes and mouth.

Asylum Kitchen

I bring more than blades or wire or shards
      of sharp glass to stir into the soup. I am at once

sustenance, flesh, fiber, my fierce self.
      My breath percolates until you grab me

by the shoulders, silence me with your lips.
      I overflow with corn and apples, make you

forget yourself like a bottle of single malt scotch.
      I will not leave you empty. I will not let you

hunger for what isn't in you to want. Tell me
      what to do with this sack of ass's jawbones:

shall we keep the beat or slay a hundred men?
      Both require rhythm. You'll want to claim me

as a prize ham, a holiday cake, as sweets
      hung from a tree. I can't swim without

your thirty minutes. Find my seam and run
      your spoon along it. I burst at the slightest touch.

Asylum Office

Sometimes I sit at my desk and hum along
       with the lights. I shut my door, breathe air

gridded into brown carpet and ceiling tiles.
       I can taste those who killed themselves

before me. In terrible voices they whisper,
       Build model ships for us. Each takes weeks to make

and minutes to set aflame. At 5:30 I race to my stop
       on 6th Avenue. Weekends I forage at stoop sales

and outdoor markets for silk. Not many people
       give away their delicates or everyone's in love.

Perhaps you prefer bridges or the home where your parents
       always listened? In the end, I couldn't ignite things

that never were. It's raining. The air is heavy
       ahead of schedule. I used to be a hummingbird

dipping its bill into everything that might be
       sweet. I hovered for hours over open cocoons.

Rise and Run, North Palm Beach, Florida, 1978

1.

If it was just the two of us in only our socks
on the living room couch then I'd bury it
under a thoughtfully chosen stone
stenciled with initials, mine or his, or with
a crude drawing of a dead man or
a phoenix or any saint bursting
into their latest resurrection.
Most of the time I want my sins
to mean something. Today I'd settle
for a switchblade and five minutes
to cut the babysitter's heart out
in order to autopsy his disease. For now:
I was his eight-year-old sidekick,
the one he made an accomplice to rape.

2.

I now understand what I was taught
is not what he learned.
I was brought up to believe
every rule has repercussions.
For example: do not molest a child,
that's one of the most basic, most sacred.
Yet people break it every day.
The many times he traced my thighs
with his fingertips haunt me
almost as much as what they led to.

3.

There are always programs
and today's teaches us to tolerate ourselves.
Whether in a church basement
off Hoyt Street or a beige room at the hospital,
the point is to be open, sharing sins
with anyone willing to listen.
We sip thin coffee, perch on metal chairs.
The organizers call it witnessing
because it implies others
available to testify on our behalf.
We're used to being judged, even in meetings
where we learn the habit of articulating
our extensive damage.
In this process Step 10 details ways
to construct a personal dictionary
where grace and grief appear on the same page.
I'll try anything as long
as I'm allowed to create language
that will save me.

4.

Certain crimes smolder in corners.
The only proof I have of this one
is my memory, no more permanent
than origami crafted out of
flash paper. Blink and it disappears.
Is there any court that convicts
on such thin evidence?
That paper swan is not a swan
it's a vulture; that paper body is not a body,
it's an ember made of ghosts.

Place my corpse next to hers, scalpel
open our flesh and the spirits
trapped inside disperse.

5.

In the months after it happened,
I might have been able to explain it better
if words hadn't been stacked syllables
trapped at the back of my throat.
To be more effective they had to follow
a precise arrangement: *We need all love is*
doesn't move the needle quite like, *Love is all we need.*
If only I'd been taught how to unknot
my tongue, how to tell the adults what we did
and why, I might not be writing this now.
Listen to my breath as I summon
a storm. How I wish the world
trembled under the weight of my tongue.

6.

Take a moment to meditate every day:
settle in a comfortable spot
and focus on a shelf with votives
or vases or if that doesn't work
try staring at swaying branches.
Breathe with purpose. Make a bellows
of your lungs, then the world.
In, out—that's all this is—in...
out. To slow your pulse
slow your thoughts; your mind
is a brook, a breeze,
the patient breath of a bluebell.

7.

I keep dreaming up stories
in which I release myself from this
but never get very far. Mornings, I find empty pints
of ice cream in the trash and don't remember
cold on my tongue. The past scares me
because the patterns never change.
Tonight, gutters sing with rain,
the same staccato *ahhs* and *ohhs*
I listened to as a kid. In Florida, rainstorms
approach from every direction and August
is a series of numbered squalls.

8.

If the events I can't stop
describing were the plot of a movie
then it would have rained that night
with thunder knocking against three horizons—
his, hers, mine. Lightning would strobe
and blind us; we'd see flashes
of townspeople hunting the villain.
In the last ten minutes they'd find him
and bring him to justice. This
isn't a movie, there was no justice.
I got lucky, she didn't. Even
after so many years when I blink
it's her eyes that flicker by,
two beams signaling
from somewhere off in the dark.

Asylum Vacation

In which saints wired upright along the walls
        bless us from their shawls and faded shrouds.

Their skulls list and lean as if remembering
        their dried tongues. I can't recall if this

is a nightmare or our vacation in Palermo,
        a crypt thick with anxious dead. These vessels

show us how we are an operating theater
        with popcorn for the show. A beetle chews

on the strings linking breast plate to spine.
        Have you read the reports? The physicists

are helpless. A man touches the thin web
        of one's hair. *Without their flesh they're the same,*

he says. Sometimes the truth is an exit ramp
        next to a gas station selling peanut brittle;

sometimes a fist of thirsty starlings circle and circle,
        a beauty we have to tilt our heads to see.

Asylum Spring

It might be April and rain. It might have
　　　　something to do with love, a peculiar form

of disease. I've never tried uneasiness
　　　　as a mating strategy, with distress as the prime

biological imperative: love the one you're
　　　　uncomfortable with. Today I'm numb and

don't know why. Same skin, same life but
　　　　this numb is different. Every night I go to bed

planning to reinvent myself come morning.
　　　　But each daylight's litany of fresh disasters

seek attention. Coffee, bagel, go to work.
　　　　Smoothie, hot tea, go to work. There's never

enough time to construct a new me, the one
　　　　where I open my eyes certain I'm ascending.

Late afternoon sleet bounces off my skin
　　　　then hovers before settling around my feet.

Faith

For centuries, an order of Japanese monks
chose one of their elders to deliver prayers
to the island of an important Boddhisattva. They set
the elect adrift in a shrine shaped like a coffin

with a month of salted fish, rice crackers and water
while brothers on shore kept watch for signs of panic.
In many cases, the sacrifice tried to row home
but the others turned him, shoved him back

into the sea. A mirror of human existence:
each of us sent to beg forgiveness from whichever
gods we recognize while death patiently paces
the sky. As darkness swallows the world, imagine

the cry of gulls, glimpses of a distant horizon,
the slow groan of a casket atop the waves.

Clearing Snow

Two trucks pushing a blizzard off the streets
remind me of jury duty. A city vehicle had crashed

into a single mom's hatchback, injured her neck.
When the lawyers asked whose side I'd take,

I told them I wanted to see evidence, said,
I thought that was the point? I've never felt

the burden of religious faith though I've always
been fascinated by monks who squat

on the same mat until they know the world, how
they find it without moving. I know where I am

by studying the planets. The way their orbits recur
confirms that in order to exist everything repeats:

tides, DNA, molecules of oxygen. I can relive
my self-imposed sentence a hundred times,

I'm always guilty. Standing alone in the cold
it never matters there were no witnesses

or that injuries have long since healed.
Charts and exhibits don't reveal the full story.

Snowflakes fall thicker as night settles in.
Another pair of plows scrapes by.

FOUR.

Asylum Prognostication

Today something somewhere's burning and
       the sky's the color of an untamed emergency.

Crowding the windows we study the smoke,
       how it resembles bones arranged in the images

of our exes. At the last session someone said
       there are wants as well as needs, passed out

pamphlets outlining their differences. They
       claimed we age into parodies of our deepest

desires and we all gasped. It means only we
       know who we'll turn into. Brochures make

vacation look easy so we paste torn-out pages
       of the lives we're supposed to return to into

scrapbooks. *Focus on the future*, they keep saying,
       as if the truth doesn't live there too. Mine

is almost finished. Rumors of summer clover
       the air. Birds dangle from threadbare clouds.

Moons

There are two moons tonight, one
almost full amongst the blanket of stars
as another floats on the surface of a pond
between lily pads and stonewort.
If we had snacks there'd be a Moon Pie,
the chocolate, wafered, marshmallow treat.
For a book club reading nineteenth-century lit,
Moonstone by Wilkie Collins. If it was the 70s,
a dozen naked rumps in bus windows,
mooning. Losing my marbles? Moonstruck.
If adherents to a specific cult, one of
Reverend Moon's Moonies. Does it look
different under a western sky, more open,
more stark, vaster perhaps? Playing cards I can
shoot the moon. With broader sight
I'd be moon-eyed. Travelling with my new bride,
we lounge under a moon laden with honey.
I pour a cup of shine and swallow the moon—
how it burns, how my breath swaggers
in my chest. It's the placebo I swear by.
How many moons have I missed?
All of them, all of them. Moonfish,
mooncalf, moonbow, moonwalk, moonroof.
I settle a horned helm atop my head,
my beard grows long and I'm Moondog,
the Viking of 6th Avenue, poet and composer
flooding Manhattan with sacred sounds.
After sundown we bask in moonlight
and tell ourselves it isn't the gift
of a watchful god, sending us
its reflected glare when we're lost
and need light to find the way.

It Can Also Mean a Type of Fish

Language is made with sounds
        and symbols. An X suggests
an ending or anonymity or

        place treasure is hidden. Meaning
requires multiple strategies
        of interpretation. I'm partial

to words that slide and shift.
        Fluke's a good one: the blade
of an anchor, a harpoon's barb,

        half of a whale's tail, but also
an accidental stroke of good luck.
        At times, I wonder: the stroke

my mom had, would we call that
        a fluke? It was certainly not on
purpose, that sharp interruption

        of blood, that inexplicable, thick
weight suddenly inside the brain.
        Every time I uttered sentences

she couldn't comprehend I saw
        her share of words sink and fade.

Asylum Ghosts

I've never known how to manage a flock,
        how to gather strays to my side. Everyone

wanders from any field where I'm in charge.
        I beg, plead, and cajole but only phantoms

stick around. I study the underworld while
        dreaming because I need to know what

to expect before I'm damned with my sins
        pinned like mittens to my sleeves. After I ghost

this earth I'll reappear with my skin in strips
        and a hive of wasps for a mouth. It'll be nice

to move without gravity's unwanted attention,
        no more needles haunting my joints. I say

the world isn't ready to meet me unburdened
        by myself but when I say *me*, please know,

I mean everyone. Your god is not my god
        is not the pale spirit of our daily crucifixion.

Span

Every Christmas a man
counts the empties
stacked along the wall
where the tree used to stand.
He calculates how many
he needs to build
the glass bridge he's drawn
plans for on coasters
and placemats. One day
he'll rush across it
into the afterlife.
No matter which heaven
or hell his loved ones
are lost in, he will
hold them if he can.
He'll ask questions
he always meant to ask.
He'll describe the lush,
cool hills, the impatient
sea, the long chain
of hollow hours.

The Walk Home

We shuffle past the sleeping brownstones
& casket factory, past the sheet metal shop

& auto repair with broken-down tour buses
stalled along one end of Union Street Bridge.

We cross the Gowanus Canal, past the lot
where food trucks leak grease & fry oil, haven

for rats. It's after midnight, closer to dawn.
At this hour the world feels like a dream.

Every fall the smashed seeds of gingko trees
coat the sidewalk, make the air smell as if

we're walking through a new epidemic,
make us struggle to breathe with ease.

It takes longer to walk home from the bar
than it did to get there and we don't know why.

Moving to the city we were told to be vigilant
at all times. We might get mugged or

something worse. Wind pushes into us
from Buttermilk Channel & New York Bay,

sails in off the burning Atlantic. It fills us
with salt & light. It means we're nearly back,

safe. We begin to relax. Our lungs expand.
We hold our breath as long as we can.

Asylum Music

You walk down a street a thousand times,
        one hand in your pocket, the other conducting

the broken chords of traffic lights. Windows
        flush with reflected sky, screens troubled

by the breeze before a front. Your frame
        remains constant: gold and chipped and carved

with measures. We know skeletons falter
        where bone meets socket, where the flutes

of our legs whistle and turn. We are full
        of the many ways bodies breach and trespass.

Note the harm your glances cause, casual
        studies of other peoples' pain. The first time

you met a burn victim you turned away,
        unable to focus on the face beneath the face.

Preparing Not to Drown

Growing up near the ocean I knew the ways
        water wanted to take me. South Florida is ever

full of hazards: canals, sinkholes, swamps,
        choppy inlets where Intracoastal meets sea.

One day in a neighbor's pool a kid pulled me
        down, held me under. Helpless, trapped, I saw

my path toward death and thrashed my way out.
        Other close calls: aged 3 at the water slide;

aged 10, pinned beneath waves by the undertow;
        7-18, untold gallons inhaled when least expected.

See, not drowning involves impossible calm.
        After the sky went silent on September 11th

everyone in New York City held their breath
        hoping to find the surface. We emerged

from subways with lungs full and went about
        our business as if we'd never need more oxygen.

I knew my throat would seal itself off if I didn't
        hunt for escape routes, didn't keep packed bags

near the door. In the weeks that followed I saw
        how gentle people could be and thought: *We share*

sidewalks, step aside when someone's choosing olives, never
        stab each other in the neck to make it easier to breathe.

Static

Verified fact: listening to the sound of running water
reduces the speed of our hearts' palpitations:

waves of waves hushing into shore, streams smoothing
the edges of stones, rain cluttering a gutter.

If I lived by the beach I'd breathe in sync with stars
and starfish, but no one's allowed to be serene

these days. Every morning I'm assaulted by news I never
wanted—family, nation, world in flames

or soon to be—and now my mind's gone wire and hay,
a radio stuck on AM at the left end of the dial.

Most of it's white noise, a steady exhalation of sighs,
the recurrent *shhhh* of dirt filling a grave.

How will I learn the words that prevent me from getting
lost inside my head when my heart's a hedge

maze too? I'm always one syllable short of morphing
from *hum* to *human*, one letter shy of keeping

dread from shifting to *dead*. I am finished pretending
any of it makes sense. If you can read this,

please, I beg you: dig me up, saw me open, feast
on anything you think can sustain you.

Asylum Pests

And now, bees in the walls. At night I nod
        into sleep while the TV warbles. Plaster

knocks against the beams behind the bricks
        and that begs causation, this followed by that—

the way California shakes when tectonic plates
        collide, the way sparks ruin whatever wants

to burn. I hear stories about people finding
        nests in the open spaces of their houses, under

eaves, in attics. For biology class we grew colonies
        of fruit flies to learn the best way to kill them:

cider vinegar with drops of soap. Oh sweet,
        sweet death: I want to wake where nothing

wants to test me, where people behave
        in ways I can ignore without breaking down.

Whatever's in the walls seems closer now. I can't wait
        till someone sets this place on fire.

Oversight

More than two thousand satellites orbit the earth
at any given moment. We rely on them
when we check scores or read texts we'd like
to pretend we never saw. They float there, bringing us
closer while recording our intimate secrets.

Satellites are a favorite target of conspiracy theorists
and if you believe what's written online, getting
a flu shot means they know your bank balance,
your childhood pet's name, what you look like naked.
They show us what we've done to the planet, too,

and I wonder, when we exhaust the supply of diamonds,
how will we signify love? How will we cut things
only diamonds can cut? We'll need the lasers. I have
tattoos I'd like removed, ones that resemble bruises. My pain
is meaningful but I don't have to live with it forever.

Everyone's searching for pristine planets we can
move to. They think a solar system this vast
and terrifying must be cluttered with viable landscapes.
Scientists beam messages to the stars hoping
for answers but the stars respond: *you're not ready, you're not
ready, somehow, in spite of everything, you're still not ready.*

Experiments with Time Travel

I find a thirty-year-old greeting card
from my friend David. While seniors in high school
he hid it inside a coat I never wore
and I found it the first time seven years after that
while piling up thrift store donations: *Hi Scott.*
I just put this in your pocket now and you just read it now
and now we are discussing it wherever
we happen to be. I'd read a theory that posited
the simultaneity of time—as in
you are being born now as you read these words
and you are also kissing the first person
willing to taste you now and dying alone
at a music festival in a field in Austria now
and your mother was born now...

In other words, it is not time that passes
but we who pass through time, our minds locked
conveyor-belt-style in a series of linear moments.
This is complicated stuff. But I needed then
to believe in a universe where things
that happened had also not yet happened,
where I am unmolested and the girl in the wrong place
on the wrong night is not taken down
by the same acne-scarred babysitter as me.
Yet if I interpret this theory literally, then those things
always happen and always haven't happened yet
and time is woven from thread
no machine can analyze and sure enough
I need to move on and quit hoping

I can conjure the key that unlocks the portal
I'll slip through back to the moment
before our joint tragedy.
If the theory was true—David thought
it was absurd and demonstrated why
using physics, math and reality—
then I suppose I am already dead
and none of it matters. And if I'm already dead
then I have wasted too much energy
feeling sorry for myself, and her, my guilt and shame
false gods I've worshipped too long.
However. On the off chance
I *am* right for once, David, then this is me
choosing to place a letter in the pocket

of a pinstripe suit you will one day wear
to a wedding or perhaps a wake.
In this letter I declare that I have finally let go,
that I have shuffled along my personal chronology
into a new awareness of the bright sky above,
easier in my gait from what I no longer need to carry.
And I weep for joy knowing
I've managed to finally shed the weight
of that single moment. Yes. In this instant I am Atlas
deciding to set the heavens down to see
what's visible from different vantages:
the lights that shine from other stars, the music
of waves, the pageant of worlds
basking in sun and plenty.

Asylum Report

The report details findings sewn into a binder,
        thread made from tongues. It describes virtual

constellations of nightmares in which a group
        of people perform impromptu surgeries

on their enemies, a scenario Bosch might have
        been afraid to put down on canvas: viscera

knived open, chests stitched to other chests,
        shoulder blades, faces. A team of experts

is building a glossary to explain the specific
        syntax of misery. In this case, agony appears

to be its own reward. The tribe's migration
        leads to the coast. After that they may have

drowned. They may have set sail and found
        shores plentiful and serene. We have no means

to verify any of this. We are sorry for your
        loss. There is no further record of the colony.

Signs

Written with a paint pen on the wall
near the hand dryer: *Never fiddle*
through joy, brother. That's at the bar
where I've served, been served, blacked out,
gotten lost, left my sunglasses behind
so many times I couldn't say when dawn
took place, just know that light eventually
erupted through Prospect Park's trees.
The man who carries a permanent marker
out for a drink is a poet of signs and sigils.
He searches for places his mark might be seen:
I pissed here, or snorted or fucked or filled
this concrete bunker on this day and you
will remember. Oh please, I remember.
I've had to clean up after him: umbrellas,
dime bags, condoms, caps, keys.
I've held his phone and resisted the urge
to selfie me doing something lewd.
It's part and parcel of owning a bar,
this taking care of the messes of others.
I don't mind, I've had to do worse.
Besides, I live a good life
and it seems a small price to pay.
Take happiness seriously wherever
you find it, in beers made from lemongrass
or cocktails with elaborate names like
Westminster champions or an eight-mile run
under the paling streetlights along
any postcard block of Park Slope, Brooklyn
where I stumble past iron-railed stoops

with my lover, my heart a burning engine,
my laser eyes scrawling proof
of the miracle of us finding each other
into every brownstone we pass. Whatever
we've lost is left behind, shed skin, shorn hair,
evidence for someone to collect, bricks on fire,
lintels reduced to cinders, bridges crossed
to get where we are now impassable.

During a Power Outage I Face the Fact I'd Last 20 Minutes Post-Apocalypse in Spite of All My Video Game Training

I've been preparing for this for forty years
yet can't even find batteries
for the flashlight. We'll power up
with protein bars and these cans of soup
bought three blizzards ago, and if we hurry
we can forage in the deli before others panic,
and I think those drops searing holes
through my shirt may be acid rain. I have
no clue where we'll find two high-tech
combat suits or cryogenic limbs, and why
is the sky scarlet and my, how the rats
have quadrupled in size.
                                    Love, I miss
your lips as they slip from your face.
There goes my hair. There goes the delicate
shell of us. Perhaps we should lie down
on this highway of rubble and ash until we hear
the wind whistle past what were our ears and,
Love, do not fear that blinking light
and high-pitched beep, that's what health
we have left before this world starts over.

After Asylum

Even then I was surrounded by walls
       needing spackle, those sainted bulwarks,

bastions of divine grievance, i.e. Holy.
       Or holey. It's Tuesday. There's no rain

slipping from awnings and the earth
       drifts far enough from the sun that I only

sweat when I make an effort. Now I have
       a jar of paste, a pair of scissors and magazines

in piles. I'll collage me into the pattern.
       No one will know what's a glittering dream

and what's me. Avoiding laundry, I can't
       walk past the graveyard or I'll think how

the coffins bloom. They want me blindfolded
       in thick fog; theaters pump it in under the seats.

Frayed landlines become strict perches.
       Pray for me, you rosaries of blackbirds.

Notes

"Oubliette": An oubliette is a secret dungeon with only one exit, a trap door at the top. Its name derives from the French *oublier*, "to forget;" "oubliette" literally means "place of forgetting."

"Devo Begs a Question": Devo's first album was called, "Q: Are We Not Men? A: We Are Devo!" released in 1978 by Warner Records, a division of Warner Bros.

"The Spoils": The first complete sentence is a group text sent from a friend, Wade Strickland. Thank you, Wade.

"Time and Tide": The lunar mountain Mons Huygens was named after the Dutch mathematician, physicist and engineer Christiaan Huygens. He patented the first pendulum clock in 1657 which quickly became the standard timepiece worldwide.

"During a Power Outage I Face the Fact I'd Last 20 Minutes Post-Apocalypse In Spite of All My Video Game Training": The title is a social media post by the poet Matthew Minicucci from the year 2018. Thank you, Matt.

ACKNOWLEDGMENTS

Thanks to the following publications in which these poems first appeared:

Alan Squire Bulletin: "Déjà Vu" and "Waking Up in Florida"
Allium Journal: "Rise and Run"
Atlanta Review: "Oversight"
Atticus Review: "During a Power Outage I Face the Fact..." and "Porch Song"
Bayou: "Wanting to Be a Fish"
Bookends: "In the Town That Talks to the Dead"
Burningword: "Aftermath"
Cagibi: "Viewer's Guide to Masculinity"
The Carolina Quarterly: "Learning to Shut Up"
Cider House Review: "Café in Early Winter"
Cloudbank: "Moons"
Coffin Bell: "Spiritual"
Comstock Review: " Experiments with Time Travel"
december: "Asylum Schedule" and "Asylum Sunday"
Denver Quarterly: "Asylum Prognostication"
Fatal Flaw Literary: "Asylum Devotion"
Freshwater Review: "Up in This Trailer Park" and "Undone"
Gigantic Sequins: "Clearing Snow"
Glassworks: "Preparing Not to Drown"
Ilanot Review: "Upstate"
Inkwell Journal: "Static"
Iron Horse Literary Revew: "Asylum: An Argument"
Jabberwock: "The Spoils"
Jet Fuel Review: "Asylum Ghosts"
Menacing Hedge: "Asylum Kitchen" and "Asylum Sleight of Hand"
Moon City Review: "Asylum Pests"
New Ohio Review: "Gothic"

The Normal School: "After Asylum" and "Signs"
Opossum: "Bottomless Cup" and "Hammerstein Ballroom"
Permafrost: "Asylum Spring"
The Pinch: "Oubliette"
Poem-A-Day: "Faith"
Poetry Northwest: "The Elephants"
Puerto del Sol Online: "Asylum Tonight" and "Asylum Vacation"
Raleigh Review: "Asylum Release"
The Rumpus: "Asylum Music," "Asylum Office," "Asylum Report" and
"Asylum Trial"
Stoneboat Literary: "Hunger, or, Excessive Sunlight Can Lead to..."
Sundog: "Hunt Camp, Labelle, FL"
Sweet Literary Confection: "It Can Also Mean a Type of Fish"
Twyckenham Notes: "Tech-Friendly Apocalypse"
Variant Literature: "Asylum Linguistics" and "Asylum Testament"
Watershed Review: "Tender"

Massive thanks to Chryss Yost and David Starkey at Gunpowder Press for saying yes and for all their hard work making this book happen. Massive thanks also to the editors of magazines who've published my poems and the helpful edits they suggested.

Thank you to my parents, Sid and Annette Stubbs, who supported and encouraged me every step of the way, with special thanks to mom for the cover art.

Thank you to my sisters, Melanie Chitwood and Natalie Isaac for their love, enthusiasm and cookies.

Thanks to the Booher and Szmukler families, especially lifelong friends Adam and David: your friendship keeps me going.

Thank you to friends who read and commented on my work at various stages: Lucy Griffith, Bob Johnson, Lisa Lynn Moore, Kerri Webster, Tyler Mills, Terence Degnan, Melanie Datz Sirof, Bob King, Steve Bellin-

Oka, Sarah McKinstry-Brown, Daniel Tierney, Jeremy Proehl and John Romagna.

Thank you to my poetry teachers: Robert Hedin, David Wojahn, Yusef Komunyakaa, Maura Stanton, Roger Mitchell, Catherine Bowman, Mark Halliday, Rowan Ricardo Phillips, A. Van Jordan, Martha Rhodes, & Patrick Phillips.

Special thanks to my cohort at Indiana for helping me find my voice: Vandana Khanna, Karen Carcia, James D'Agostino, David Daniels, and Sass Brown. Thanks also to IU friends who listened and offered advice: Tenaya Darlington, Karen Heath, Dobby Gibson, Chris Foley, Angela Pneuman and Christine Sneed.

Thank you to the Bread Loaf Writers' Conference for supporting my work and for the amazing people I met there, especially: Jennifer Grotz, Lauren Francis-Sharma, Noreen Cargill, Jason Lamb, and Hope Snyder. Special thanks to the staff from 2022 and 2023 for putting up with me and my hip. Shout-out to the original Burdick boys, Stephen Fishbach, Tom Manella, Eric Simpson and Sanjay Agnihotri: thank you for staying calm through the moth incident.

Massive thanks to Mike and Ben Wiley, our co-owners in Mission Dolores, whose energy, generosity and friendship allowed me the space to get back to writing poems.

Special thanks, as always, to the Moes.

Thank you to anyone I've failed to list here, and my heartiest apologies.

Finally, thank you to my wife Margaret O'Connor for being the most encouraging, supporting, loving, cheer-leading partner a man could ever hope for. None of this happens without you.

About the Poet

SM Stubbs lives in Brooklyn, NY, where he and his wife co-owned a craft-beer bar. Born and raised in South Florida, he attended Wake Forest and then Indiana University where he acquired his MFA. He was the recipient of a scholarship to and on staff at Bread Loaf Writers' Conference and was nominated for the Pushcart Prize and Best New Poets. His work has appeared in *Poetry Northwest, Poem-A-Day, New Ohio Review, december, Iron Horse, The Rumpus, Crab Creek Review, Cagibi, Anacapa Review* and elsewhere.

ALSO FROM

GUNPOWDER PRESS

Empty Me Full, poems by Catherine Abbey Hodges
Frangible Operas, poems by Susan Kelly-DeWitt
Before Traveling to Alabama, poems by David Case
Mother Lode, poems by Peg Quinn
Raft of Days, poems by Catherine Abbey Hodges
Unfinished City, poems by Nan Cohen
Original Face, poems by Jim Peterson
Shaping Water, poems by Barry Spacks
The Tarnation of Faust, poems by David Case
Mouth & Fruit, poems by Chryss Yost

CALIFORNIA POETS SERIES

In Praise of Late Wonder, poems by Lee Herrick
Downtime, poems by Gary Soto
Speech Crush, poems by Sandra McPherson
Our Music, poems by Dennis Schmitz
Gatherer's Alphabet, poems by Susan Kelly-DeWitt

DRYDEN-VREELAND BOOK PRIZE

Three-Day Weekend, poems by Christopher Blackman

BARRY SPACKS POETRY PRIZE

In the Cathedral of My Undoing, poems by Kellam Ayres
Accidental Garden, poems by Catherine Esposito Prescott
Like All Light, poems by Todd Copeland
Curriculum, poems by Meghan Dunn
Drinking with O'Hara, poems by Glenn Freeman
The Ghosts of Lost Animals, poems by Michelle Bonczek Evory
Posthumous Noon, poems by Aaron Baker
Burning Down Disneyland, poems by Kurt Olsson
Instead of Sadness, poems by Catherine Abbey Hodges

ALTA CALIFORNIA CHAPBOOKS

Alba and Other Songs, poems by Fred Arroyo
The First Amelia, poems by Amelia Rodriguez
On Display, poems by Gabriel Ibarra
Sor Juana, poems by Florencia Milito
Levitations, poems by Nicholas Reiner
Grief Logic, poems by Crystal AC Salas

FULL CATALOG AT GUNPOWDERPRESS.COM